PRAYER

THAT

MAKES

ENEMIES SURRENDER

By Tella Olayeri

08023583168

Published By:

GOD'S LINK VENTURES

Email tellaolayeri@gmail.com

Website http://tellaolayeri.com

US Contact
Ruth Jack
14 Milewood Road
Verbank
N.Y.12585
U.S.A. +19176428989

DEDICATION

This book is dedicated to the **HOLY GHOST** for inspiring me to write this eye opening book.

APPRECIATION

My appreciation goes to my dedicated wife, **MRS NGOZI OLAYERI,** who typed the manuscript of this book and designed the cover page. My darling wife I say thank you. My appreciation equally goes to my lovely children, **MISS IBUKUN, DAVID, MICHAEL COMFORT and MERCY.** They encouraged me day and night as I write this book

Respect and honor should be given to who is due. Favor comes from God and men as well. My calling (writing evangelism) met the timely support of a particular man of God, preacher, teacher, prophet and General Overseer. He awakes my inner man and gave me sound spiritual support. Without his earlier support for my first book, *Fire for Fire Prayer Book* and subsequent ones, I may not be where I am today in Christian literature writing. He gallantly stood by me in fulfillment of my calling.

This book you are holding is a testimony of my claim. This book wouldn't have seen the light of the day, if not for the spiritual encouragement I gathered from my father in the Lord who served as spiritual mirror that brightens my hope to explore my calling.

I am talking of no any other person than the **General Overseer of MOUNTAIN OF FIRE**

AND MIRACLES MINISTRIES WORLD WIDE, DR. D. K. OLUKOYA.

Once again, I say thank you sir. Your support has yielded yet another earth shaking book.
THANKS
Evangelist Tella Olayeri.

PREFACE

It is time we rise up in prayer and stop enemies that rise to cause sorrow in our life. Witchcraft powers are not ready to slow down or quit in their acts. They are wicked and heartless in wickedness, no wonder the phrase, "Wickedly wicked with wickedness" is often used to describe them. If a power is wickedly wicked, what do you expect? The answer is wickedness, terror, sorrow, brutality, hunger, famine, poverty, anger, closed door to progress and prosperity.

This book is written to set the captives free from the grip of higher power of Satan and his cohorts. Really, you are not a captive, but circumstances and challenges you face makes you victim in the hands of the wicked. This tells us, we are in battle field. There is no one born of flesh that does not experience one battle or the other. This is the more reason, you must pray to make enemies surrender and quit your life.

To achieve this, this book analyse every issue in prayer. It makes God first in the book. It reveals to us how important the covenant of God is to us. The book treats in prayer our covenant with God. He is always there to answer us whenever we call on him. Our covenant with God through father Abraham is to succeed in life and have peace. This is what enemies are against. The bottom line is, they won't succeed in their adventure against you. No filthy language from their mouth shall pull you down. The Lord shall establish kindness, mercy and love to you. It is time to pray and excel.

This book is loaded with prayer to pursue, to overtake and recover all. It proofs you are not a failure and shall not be, as you lay hands on this book. All closed doors of breakthrough shall open. Days of losses are gone; it is now to count your blessings in the Lord. As you pray with this book, the Lord shall pour anointing oil of breakthrough upon you. Evil doers in your environment shall be silenced, as you stay fresh and green. Dark powers that surround you shall be seen no more. At the end, the Lord shall give you rest from the enemy.

Brethren, it is time you pray and occupy your Canaan Land. Take bold step, buy this book and pray. May the LORD Almighty give you strength to pray. I assure you; every enemy that rises up against you shall fail and surrender, in the name of Jesus. Amen.

GOOD NEWS!!!

My audiobook is now available, to get one visit acx.com and search **"Tella Olayeri."**

Brethren, to be loaded and reloaded visit: *amazon.com/author/tellaolayeri* for a full spiritual sojourn for my books.

Thanks.

PREVIOUS PUBLICATIONS OF THE AUTHOR

1. 100% CONFESSIONS and PROPHECIES to Locate Helpers and helpers to locate you
2. 1000 Prayer Points for Children Breakthrough
3. 1010 (One Thousand and Ten) DREAMS and Interpretations
4. 2000 Dangerous Prayer for First Born
5. 365 DREAMS and INTERPRETATIONS
6. 430 Prayers to Cancel Bad Dreams and Overcome Witchcraft Powers part one (DREAMS AND YOU Book 1)
7. 430 Prayers to Claim Good Dreams and Overcome Witchcraft Powers part two (DREAMS AND YOU Book 2)
8. 630 Acidic Prayers: With Missile Prayer for Speedy Breakthrough, Healing and Deliverance
9. 650 DREAMS AND INTERPRETATIONS
10. 700 Prayers to Clear Unemployment Out of Your Way
11. 720 Missile Prayers that Silence Enemies: Prayers that Bring Peace and Rest
12. 740 Rocket Prayers that Break Satanic Embargo
13. 777 Deliverance Prayers for Healing and Breakthrough
14. 800 Deliverance Prayer for Middle Born: Daily Devotional for Teen and Adult

See all at: amazon.com/author/tellaolayeri

Table of Contents

CHAPTER 1

LET COVENANT OF GOD REIGN

Colossians 3:5-10

5. Put to death, therefore, whatever belongs to your earthly nature: sexual immorality, impurity, lust, evil desires and greed, which is idolatry.

6. Because of these, the wrath of God is coming.

7. You used to walk in these ways, in the life you once lived.

8. But now you must also rid yourselves of all such things as these: anger, rage, malice, slander, and filthy language from your lips.

9. Do not lie to each other, since you have taken off your old self with its practices

10. And have put on the new self, which is being renewed in knowledge in the image of its Creator.

Isaiah 60:1-5

1. "Arise, shine, for your light has come, and the glory of the LORD rises upon you.

2. See, darkness covers the earth and thick darkness is over the peoples, but the LORD rises upon you and his glory appears over you.

3. Nations will come to your light, and kings to the brightness of your dawn.

4. "Lift up your eyes and look about you: All assemble and come to you; your sons come from afar, and your daughters are carried on the hip.

5. Then you will look and be radiant, your heart will throb and swell with joy; the wealth on the seas will be brought to you, to you the riches of the nations will come.

Jeremiah 31:33-34

33. "This is the covenant I will make with the people of Israel after that time," declares the LORD. "I will put my law in their minds and write it on their hearts. I will be their God, and they will be my people.

34. No longer will they teach their neighbor, or say to one another, 'Know the LORD,' because they will all know me, from the least of them to the greatest," declares the LORD. "For I will forgive their wickedness and will remember their sins no more."

PRAYER POINTS

1. I thank God for all his wonderful acts and works in the name of Jesus

2. I thank my God, who will continually protect me from arrow of darkness in the name of Jesus.

3. I thank my God; he shall arise and break every dark covenant that binds me to failure in the name of Jesus.

4. I thank my God that will not forsake me to the enemy in the name of Jesus.

5. I thank my God who gives all good things of life in the name of Jesus.

6. O Lord, I thank you, for you give peace and mercy to all who keep your covenant in the name of Jesus.

7. O Lord, forgive me the sins that bind my soul to evil covenant in the name of Jesus.

8. O Lord, do not let sin have dominion over my life, in the name of Jesus.

9. The sins of my parents shall not bury my talent in the name of Jesus.

10. O Lord, forgive me sins that promote evil arrow in my life in the name of Jesus.

11. O Lord, have mercy upon me, set me free today in the name of Jesus.

12. Lord Jesus, don't look elsewhere, have mercy upon me today.

13.I drink blood of Jesus, to purge me of evil deposit in my body, in the name of Jesus.

14.I am covered with blood of Jesus, against evil attack in the name of Jesus.

15.I am an overcomer through the blood of Jesus.

16.I am redeemed by the blood of Jesus.

17.Blood of Jesus, separate me from evil covenant, in the name of Jesus.

18.Blood of Jesus, nullify blood covenant troubling my soul in the name of Jesus.

19.Holy Spirit nullify covenant that put me in bondage, in the name of Jesus.

20.Holy Spirit, lay hands upon me so that I can speak against unfruitful covenants ravaging my life in the name of Jesus.

21.Holy Spirit, be my mentor and saviour in the name of Jesus.

22.Holy Ghost Power, break covenants from pit of hell, troubling my soul in the name of Jesus.

23.Lord Jesus, fill me with fresh outpouring of Holy Ghost in the name of Jesus.

24.O Lord, send down fire of revival for signs and wonders in my life in the name of Jesus.

25.Lord Jesus, give me dominion, let me possess and use it, to glorify your name in the name of Jesus.

26. O Lord, make me complete in you, so that enemy may not disgrace me in the name of Jesus.

27. O Lord, I am here, let prosperity covenant of father Abraham reign in my life, in the name of Jesus.

28. I put to death every earthly thing that will not let me see the face of God, in the name of Jesus.

29. Every covenant with sexual immorality, break in the name of Jesus.

30. Every covenant with evil desire in my life, break in the name of Jesus.

31. Covenant with power of my father's house, break in the name of Jesus.

32. Spirit of anger in my life, quit my life and die, in the name of Jesus.

33. Malice spirit in me, kicking against Godly spirit in me, I chase you out of me, in the name of Jesus.

34. Every filthy language in my mouth, not promoting God, expire in the name of Jesus.

35. Lying spirit in me, kicking against Godly spirit in me I chase you out of me, in the name of Jesus.

36. I put off old habits in me and put on God's way of life, in the name of Jesus.

37. Jesus Christ of Nazareth, arrest me to you, in the name of Jesus.

38. I am God's chosen, not Satan, in the name of Jesus.

39. I clothe myself with compassion, instead of hatred in the name of Jesus.

40. O Lord, establish spirit of kindness and humility in my life, in the name of Jesus.

41. O Lord, establish spirit of gentleness and patience in me in the name of Jesus.

42. Lord Jesus, let your peace reign in my life in the name of Jesus.

43. O Lord, deposit in my heart, ability to sing Psalms, hymns and spiritual songs, in the name of Jesus.

44. O Lord, put your law in my mind and write it in my heart, in the name of Jesus.

45. O Lord, be my God and I will be your child in the name of Jesus.

46. O Lord, establish yourself in my family, in the name of Jesus.

47. O Lord, establish your covenant with me, I will not break it, in the name of Jesus.

48. I will arise and shine in the covenant of the Lord, in the name of Jesus.

49. Power of darkness quit my life, for light of God to reign in my life, in the name of Jesus.

50. Glory of God, appear in my life, in the name of Jesus.

51. O Lord, let your covenant with me, bring light to my life, in the name of Jesus.

52. O Lord, let your covenant with me, bring nobles and kings to me in the name of Jesus.

53. Heavenly joy, fill my heart, in the name of Jesus.

54. Lord Jesus, change bad report of me to good report, so that I may have upper hand against my enemy in the name of Jesus.

55. O Lord, give me mountain moving faith to break every covenant that does not promote your name in the name of Jesus.

56. O Lord, let your armour empower me against principalities and powers, in the name of Jesus.

57. Lord Jesus, make me sensitive to your voice and command, in the name of Jesus.

58. I walk back from the path that lead to the spirits of the dead, in the name of Jesus.

59. Holy Ghost, withdraw my name and identity from the book of oppressors, in the name of Jesus.

60. O Lord, put an end to every covenant of impossibility and failure in my life, in the name of Jesus.

61. O Lord, break and refill me afresh for your exploits, in the name of Jesus.
62. O Lord, save me from powers that holds my soul to captivity in the name of Jesus.
63. O Lord, let arrow assign to scatter my hope, break in the name of Jesus.
64. O Lord, remove every hindrance on my way, caused by evil arrow in the name of Jesus.
65. O Lord, break every covenant with lust spirit in my life, in the name of Jesus.
66. Every covenant that leads to quarrel in my home break in the name of Jesus.
67. Every covenant that bring darkness to my life, break in the name of Jesus.
68. O Lord, scatter the plan of the enemy against my life, in the name of Jesus.
69. O Lord, dismantle works of Satan in my life, in the name of Jesus.
70. Spirit of lust introduced to my life to break the covenant I have with God, come out of me in the name of Jesus.
71. My head, reject covenant of failure, in the name of Jesus.
72. My body reject covenant of sickness, in the name of Jesus.
73. My hands reject covenant of poverty, in the name of Jesus.

74. I break myself loose from covenant of stagnation, in the name of Jesus.
75. I break myself loose from evil association covenant, in the name of Jesus.
76. I break and destroy every witchcraft covenant I did in my place of birth, in the name of Jesus.
77. I break and destroy every negative blood covenant, in the name of Jesus.

CHAPTER 2

I SHALL NOT BE NAKED

Genesis 28:12-18

12. *He had a dream in which he saw a stairway resting on the earth, with its top reaching to heaven, and the angels of God were ascending and descending on it.*

13. There above it stood the LORD, and he said: "I am the LORD, the God of your father Abraham and the God of Isaac. I will give you and your descendants the land on which you are lying.

14. Your descendants will be like the dust of the earth, and you will spread out to the west and to the east, to the north and to the south. All peoples on earth will be blessed through you and your offspring.

15. I am with you and will watch over you wherever you go, and I will bring you back to this land. I will not leave you until I have done what I have promised you."

16. When Jacob awoke from his sleep, he thought, "Surely the LORD is in this place, and I was not aware of it."

17. He was afraid and said, "How awesome is this place! This is none other than the house of God; this is the gate of heaven."

18. Early the next morning Jacob took the stone he had placed under his head and set it up as a pillar and poured oil on top of it.

Psalm 92:9-14

9. For surely your enemies, LORD, surely your enemies will perish; all evildoers will be scattered.

10. You have exalted my horn like that of a wild ox; fine oils have been poured on me.

11. My eyes have seen the defeat of my adversaries; my ears have heard the rout of my wicked foes.

12. The righteous will flourish like a palm tree, they will grow like a cedar of Lebanon;

13. Planted in the house of the LORD, they will flourish in the courts of our God.

14. They will still bear fruit in old age, they will stay fresh and green,

1 Samuel 30:3-8

3. When David and his men reached Ziklag, they found it destroyed by fire and their wives and sons and daughters taken captive.

4. So David and his men wept aloud until they had no strength left to weep.

5. David's two wives had been captured Ahinoam of Jezreel and Abigail, the widow of Nabal of Carmel.

6. David was greatly distressed because the men were talking of stoning him; each one was bitter in spirit because of his sons and daughters. But David found strength in the LORD his God.

7. Then David said to Abiathar the priest, the son of Ahimelek, "Bring me the ephod." Abiathar brought it to him,

8. And David inquired of the LORD, "Shall I pursue this raiding party? Will I overtake them?" "Pursue them," he answered. "You will certainly overtake them and succeed in the rescue."

PRAYER POINTS

1. I thank you Lord, for you shall silence spirit of nakedness in my life in the name of Jesus.
2. I thank my God, who put new song in my mouth in the name of Jesus.

3. I thank God, who will make me dance my dance and be filled with joy in the name of Jesus.
4. I thank my God, who remove rags from me and wear me new garment in the name of Jesus.
5. I thank my God, who says, I will not cry or be in sober mood in the name of Jesus.
6. I thank my God, who shall make me great in life in the name of Jesus.
7. Lord Jesus, forgive me so that I can forge ahead in life in the name of Jesus.
8. O Lord, forgive me when I raise my hands unto you in prayer, when I backslide forgive me, in the name of Jesus.
9. Lord Jesus, have mercy upon me, wear me with garment of breakthrough in the name of Jesus.
10. Lord Jesus, have mercy upon me, wear me with garment of breakthrough in the name of Jesus.
11. O Lord, forgive me every sin that may give enemy in road to my life in the name of Jesus.
12. O Lord, let your forgiveness be total so that enemy may not have advantage over me in the name of Jesus.
13. I plead blood of Jesus over my life in the name of Jesus.
14. Blood of Jesus, cover my nakedness in the name of Jesus.

15.I cover myself with blood of Jesus, to stop attacks against my person in the name of Jesus.

16.I drink blood of Jesus, to strengthen me against powers that vow to naked me in the name of Jesus.

17.Blood of Jesus, put smile in my face in the name of Jesus.

18.By the power in the blood of Jesus, I am covered with garment of peace in the name of Jesus.

19.Holy Spirit, I am for you, accept me by fire, in the name of Jesus.

20.Holy Spirit, take me through to palace of greatness in the name of Jesus.

21.Holy Ghost Power, save me from the hand of spirit of nakedness in the name of Jesus.

22.Holy Spirit, lay hands of breakthrough on my head in the name of Jesus.

23.Holy Spirit, cover my nakedness from evil attack in the name of Jesus.

24.Lord Jesus, do not take Holy Spirit, from me, I don't want to be naked in the name of Jesus.

25.O Lord, open way to run to you as a strong tower, in the name of Jesus.

26.O Lord, give me mountain moving faith to speak against nakedness assign to rubbish me, in the name of Jesus.

27. O Lord, let our angels ascend and descend for my sake in the name of Jesus.

28. Angels of God, arise see to my plight, cover my nakedness, in the name of Jesus.

29. O Lord, give me my inheritance, in the name of Jesus.

30. O Lord, bless me beyond my imagination, in the name of Jesus.

31. God of Abraham, God of Isaac, resurrect my destiny to fabulous prosperity in the name of Jesus.

32. Powers assigned to naked me in my sleep, die, in the name of Jesus.

33. O Lord, support me and my generations to come in the name of Jesus.

34. My name and generation shall spread out great, in the name of Jesus.

35. O Lord, let people of the earth be blessed through me, I am Abraham's seed by conversion, in the name of Jesus.

36. O Lord, watch over me wherever I go, in the name of Jesus.

37. Thou gate of heaven, open and bless me, in the name of Jesus.

38. O Lord, pour fine oil upon me to experience breakthrough wherever I turn, in the name of Jesus.

39. O Lord, let enemies against my breakthrough be silence forever in the name of Jesus.

40. Evil doers in my environment be silenced and be out in shame, in the name of Jesus.

41. O Lord, let my eyes see the defeat of my adversaries, in the name of Jesus.

42. Angels of God, rout out the wicked in the corridor of my life, in the name of Jesus.

43. I shall flourish like palm tree, in the name of Jesus.

44. O Lord, empower me to dwell in your house and presence, forever, in the name of Jesus.

45. I will stay fresh and green even in old age, in the name of Jesus.

46. Dark powers that surround me in order to naked me, be silenced in the name of Jesus.

47. Every bond of wickedness that surround me, scatter in the name of Jesus.

48. Every wound in my body, be healed by the power in the blood of Jesus.

49. O Lord, give me rest from all my enemies, in the name of Jesus.

50. Every raiding band assigned to silence me, scatter in the name of Jesus.

51. I pursue, I conquer, I recover all, in the name of Jesus.

52. O Lord, let no plot of the enemy against me stand, in the name of Jesus.
53. Lord Jesus, be my defender all the time, so that I may be victorious in what I do in the name of Jesus.
54. Lord Jesus, you are my Rock, protect me in the name of Jesus.
55. Lord Jesus, set me free from bondage of darkness in the name of Jesus.
56. O Lord, cover my nakedness, supply me all my needs according to your riches in heaven in the name of Jesus.
57. O Lord, give me abundance in every area of life, in the name of Jesus.
58. O Lord, clear away darkness that surrounds me, in the name of Jesus.
59. O Lord, restore to me the years the locust has eaten, in the name of Jesus.
60. O Lord, restore to me the years the palmerworm and caterpillar has eaten, in the name of Jesus.
61. O Lord, make your face shine upon me so that I may reap miracles in my life in the name of Jesus.
62. O Lord, pour upon me and upon my affairs, spirit of mercy and grace, in the name of Jesus.

63. O Lord, be my father that raise the poor out of the dust, and lift the needy out of the dunghill in the name of Jesus.

64. O Lord, listen to me and deliver me speedily in the name of Jesus.

65. Those who boast I will go and not return to path of life, you are a liar, die in the name of Jesus.

66. O Lord, disgrace powers intimidating my progress, in the name of Jesus.

67. Lord Jesus, bring curse of nakedness to an end in my life in the name of Jesus.

68. O Lord, let new things begin to break forth in my life in the name of Jesus.

69. By the power of the living God, no counsel of the wicked shall stand against me, in the name of Jesus.

70. Every whirlwind on evil mission to naked me, scatter, in the name of Jesus.

71. River of nakedness flowing into my life, dry up, in the name of Jesus.

72. Power of darkness that settled down in my home, your time is up, rise up walk out of my house and die in the name of Jesus.

73. Rage of witchcraft, assigned to terminate my prosperity, stop, in the name of Jesus.

74. Friends of darkness coming to me as children of light, be exposed and be disgraced, in the name of Jesus.

75. Satanic prophecy of nakedness from my father's house, against my life, backfire and scatter in the name of Jesus.

CHAPTER 3

O LORD LET SPIRITUAL BONDAGE BREAK

1 John 1:8-10

8. If we claim to be without sin, we deceive ourselves and the truth is not in us.

9. If we confess our sins, he is faithful and just and will forgive us our sins and purify us from all unrighteousness.

10. If we claim we have not sinned, we make him out to be a liar and his word is not in us.

Psalm 23:1-4

1. The LORD is my shepherd, I lack nothing.

2. He makes me lie down in green pastures, he leads me beside quiet waters,

3. He refreshes my soul. He guides me along the right paths for his name's sake.

4. Even though I walk through the darkest valley, I will fear no evil, for you are with me; your rod and your staff, they comfort me.

Psalm 26:4-12

4. I do not sit with the deceitful, nor do I associate with hypocrites.

5. I abhor the assembly of evildoers and refuse to sit with the wicked.

6. I wash my hands in innocence, and go about your altar, LORD,

7. Proclaiming aloud your praise and telling of all your wonderful deeds.

8. LORD, I love the house where you live, the place where your glory dwells.

9. Do not take away my soul along with sinners, my life with those who are bloodthirsty,

10. in whose hands are wicked schemes, whose right hands are full of bribes.

11. I lead a blameless life; deliver me and be merciful to me.

12. My feet stand on level ground; in the great congregation I will praise the LORD.

PRAYER POINTS

1. I thank God who breaks every manner of spiritual bondage in my life in the name of Jesus.
2. I thank you Lord, for you shall not leave me to the hands of darkness in the name of Jesus.
3. I thank God for his protection over me, without you I will be in permanent bondage in the name of Jesus.
4. I thank God, for he is there for me always in the name of Jesus.
5. I thank God who showers me with love and prosperity in the name of Jesus.
6. I thank my God for silencing the foes and arch enemies of my soul in the name of Jesus.
7. Lord Jesus, stretch your hand of mercy upon my head so that I may move forward in life in the name of Jesus.
8. Lord Jesus, have mercy on me, come quickly to my situation in the name of Jesus.
9. Lord Jesus, have mercy on me, rebuke every indiscipline spirit in me in the name of Jesus.
10. Lord Jesus, have mercy on me, so that I will not be hated without no reason in the name of Jesus.
11. Lord Jesus, forgive me, so that shame and confusion will not have space in my life in the name of Jesus.

12. Lord Jesus, be my comforter all the time in the name of Jesus.
13. Blood of Jesus, cleanse every identification mark in my body that attracts spirit of slavery to my life in the name of Jesus.
14. Blood of Jesus, don't abandon me, save me from hook of bondage in the name of Jesus.
15. Blood of Jesus, protect my glory and destiny from evil arrow in the name of Jesus.
16. Blood of Jesus, be a barricade between me and poverty in the name of Jesus.
17. I cover myself with blood of Jesus, peace shall reign in my life in the name of Jesus.
18. I drink blood of Jesus, for strength and vitality to ease me of bondage in the name of Jesus.
19. Holy Spirit, baptize me with fire and be there for me all the time in the name of Jesus.
20. Holy Spirit, fight this battle for me, in the name of Jesus.
21. Holy Spirit, break every chain of darkness limiting my joy in the name of Jesus.
22. Holy Spirit, break every bondage that held me captive for so long in the name of Jesus.
23. Holy Spirit, renew my eyes to see supernatural above others in the name of Jesus.
24. Holy Spirit, renew my inner man day by day, to pray and excel in life, in the name of Jesus.

25. O God, arise anoint me with anointing of excellence, in the name of Jesus.

26. Lord Jesus, set me free from every manner of bondage, for whoever you set free, is free indeed in the name of Jesus.

27. Bondage of sin, keeping me in the hand of Satan, break in the name of Jesus.

28. Bondage of sin, keeping me far from God, break and release me, in the name of Jesus.

29. Every spiritual bondage holding me back to access good things of life, break in the name of Jesus.

30. Lord Jesus, forgive me and purify me from all unrighteousness, in the name of Jesus.

31. I am a liar O Lord, if I say I do not sin, I am in bondage of sin, forgive me and break the bondage, in the name of Jesus.

32. Word of God; break every bondage I am lurked in, in the name of Jesus.

33. O Lord, you are my Shepard, lead me out of spiritual bondage holding me back from God in the name of Jesus.

34. O Lord my Shepard, speak heavenly language I will understand and set me free, in the name of Jesus.

35. O Lord my Shepherd, let me enjoy relationship with you, in the name of Jesus.

36.My God that makes me lie down in green pasture shall give me rest and free me from sorrow in the name of Jesus.

37.My God leads me beside the still waters and refreshes my soul from bondage of thirst, in the name of Jesus.

38.My God restores my soul, he heals me of bad health, I am made whole in Christ, in the name of Jesus.

39.O Lord you are Great, you gave me heavenly guidance as you lead me in the path of righteousness, in the name of Jesus.

40.I thank my God who breaks spiritual bondage of death upon me, in the name of Jesus.

41.Rod of God, break every spiritual bondage that held me captive, in the name of Jesus.

42.Heavenly hope, break every bondage of hopelessness in my life in the name of Jesus.

43.Power of faith, take over my destiny and release me of spirit of unfaithfulness, in the name of Jesus.

44.O Lord, break my bondage with hypocrites I consort with in the name of Jesus.

45.O Lord, help me, let my association in the assembly of evildoers, break, in the name of Jesus.

46. O Lord, break the bondage of sitting with the wicked, in the name of Jesus.

47. O Lord, I wash my hands in innocence and worship you, let spiritual bondage with Satan break, in the name of Jesus.

48. O Lord, live in me, so that I may live your house, in the name of Jesus.

49. O Lord, separate my soul from the soul of sinners in the name of Jesus.

50. Every wicked scheme in my hand, I discard you today, in the name of Jesus.

51. Evils in my hands that keep me in bondage I reject you, break away in the name of Jesus.

52. O Lord, pull me out of hidden place enemy placed me, in the name of Jesus.

53. O Lord, sustain me by your strong arm of protection, in the name of Jesus.

54. O Lord, curse my enemy and cut them off, in the name of Jesus.

55. O Lord, put an end to plans of people that plot evil on their bed to destroy me, in the name of Jesus.

56. O Lord, give me the desire of my heart, in the name of Jesus.

57. O Lord, show me love above my enemy, in the name of Jesus.

58. Like withered grass in the desert, so shall my enemy wither away in the name of Jesus

59. Those that envy me, be silenced, in the name of Jesus.

60. Evil doers around me, fall, and rise no more, in the name of Jesus.

61. Holy Ghost, paralyze the hand of the wicked that seized me to bondage, in the name of Jesus.

62. Holy Ghost, direct the foot of the enemy elsewhere, in the name of Jesus.

63. O Lord, let me enjoy fountain of life, in the name of Jesus.

64. O Lord, remove my soul from bondage, in the name of Jesus.

65. Every chain of wickedness assign against me break in the name of Jesus.

66. O Lord, remove your mercy and love from powers that hate my growth in the name of Jesus.

67. Lord Jesus, rebuke those who do wrong to affect me in the name of Jesus.

68. Lord Jesus, silence principalities and powers that kept me in bondage in the name of Jesus.

69. O Lord, safe me from the valley, move me to mountain top, in the name of Jesus.

70. Satanic wall build around my destiny to stop it from prospering, I pull you down in the name of Jesus.

71. O Lord, destroy and scatter the works of enemy that seek to take my life, in the name of Jesus.

72. O Lord, silence every power and personalities that seek to take my life, and put me to shame and confusion in the name of Jesus.

73. O Lord, safe me from the hands of the enemy that vow I will die in this condition in the name of Jesus.

74. Every act of the enemy that makes my heart fail, die in the name of Jesus.

75. Every trouble that surrounds me scatter, in the name of Jesus.

CHAPTER 4

THE WICKED SHALL RISE NO MORE

Zephaniah 1:15-17

15. *That day will be a day of wrath a day of distress and anguish, a day of trouble and ruin, a day of darkness and gloom, a day of clouds and blackness*

16. *A day of trumpet and battle cry against the fortified cities and against the corner towers.*

17. *I will bring such distress on all people that they will grope about like those who are blind, because they have sinned against the LORD. Their blood will be poured out like dust and their entrails like dung.*

Amos 2:13-14

13. *Now then, I will crush you as a cart crushes when loaded with grain.*

14. *The swift will not escape, the strong will not muster their strength, and the warrior will not save his life.*

Psalm 3:5-8

5. I lie down and sleep; I wake again, because the LORD sustains me.

6. I will not fear though tens of thousands assail me on every side.

7. Arise, LORD! Deliver me, my God! Strike all my enemies on the jaw; break the teeth of the wicked.

8. From the LORD comes deliverance. May your blessing be on your people.

PRAYER POINTS

1. I thank you Lord, for the wicked shall rise no more in the name of Jesus.
2. I thank my God who makes me victorious upon my enemies in the name of Jesus.
3. I thank my God who will load me with prayer to silence my enemy in the name of Jesus.
4. I thank my God for he shall scatter the plan of the enemy in the name of Jesus.
5. I thank God for his protection upon me and my family in the name of Jesus.
6. I thank you Jesus, for you are Lord of lords and King of kings in the name of Jesus.

7. O Lord, have mercy upon me, in the name of Jesus.

8. Lord Jesus, forgive me the sins I commit that does not allow my star to shine in the name of Jesus.

9. Lord Jesus, lay hands of forgiveness upon me and make me whole, within and without in the name of Jesus.

10. Lord Jesus, save my eyes from sin of lust in the name of Jesus.

11. Lord Jesus, save my ears from sin of anger and evil in the name of Jesus.

12. Lord Jesus, save my legs from sin, of visiting wrong places that don't add value to Christ in the name of Jesus.

13. I drink blood of Jesus, to give me power to subdue my enemy in the name of Jesus.

14. I drink blood of Jesus, to purge and strengthen me in the walks of life in the name of Jesus.

15. I drink blood of Jesus, to give me strength and wrestle dark forces to submission in the name of Jesus.

16. I cover myself with blood of Jesus, to serve as mark and identity that fear no evil power in the name of Jesus.

17. I cover myself with blood of Jesus, to attract goodness to my life in the name of Jesus.

18. Blood of Jesus, reverse every curse pronounced against me in the name of Jesus.

19. Holy Spirit, make way for me where it seems there is no way in the name of Jesus.

20. Holy Spirit, equip me with heavenly fire, to rise above unbelievers around me in the name of Jesus.

21. Holy Spirit, anoint my eyes to see hidden treasures and riches in the name of Jesus.

22. Holy Spirit, save me from walk of endless journey in the name of Jesus.

23. Holy Spirit, save me from powers that create crisis in the name of Jesus.

24. Holy Spirit, restore my past glory, in the name of Jesus.

25. O Lord, let the wicked be ashamed and let them be silent in the grave forever, in the name of Jesus.

26. O Lord, cut off the wicked that plan injustice against me, in the name of Jesus.

27. Arise O Lord, strike my enemies on the jaw and let them rise no more, in the name of Jesus.

28. Arise O Lord; break the teeth of the wicked and let them rise no more, in the name of Jesus.

29. Power of deliverance that will make me be the head and not the tail be my portion, in the name of Jesus.

30. The blessing of the Lord is upon me, hence, the wicked shall rise no more, in the name of Jesus.
31. Dark forces advancing after my life, scatter and rise no more in the name of Jesus.
32. Thunder of God, strike and scatter evil assembly against my soul, in the name of Jesus.
33. Those that rise up against me, scatter in the name of Jesus.
34. Those that say God shall not deliver me shall fail woefully, in the name of Jesus.
35. When the Lord raise up my head above the enemies, they shall faint, fall and rise no more, in the name of Jesus.
36. When I lie down and sleep in peace, the wicked shall fall and rise no more, in the name of Jesus.
37. When the light of God shine on my face, the wicked shall fall and rise no more, in the name of Jesus.
38. When God is merciful to me and hear my prayer, my enemy shall hear of it and rise no more in the name of Jesus.
39. When enemies surround me, they shall fall and rise no more in the name of Jesus.
40. Rulers of darkness shall fail woefully over my situation, in the name of Jesus.
41. Let trouble and ruin take over the camp of my enemy in the name of Jesus.

42. Let enemy of my soul flee naked in the name of Jesus.

43. Horsemen of darkness shall fall in their evil trade, in the name of Jesus.

44. O Lord, let the stranger not muster their strength, let them paralyse, and rise no more, in the name of Jesus.

45. Enemies whose throats are open grave against me, shall rise no more, in the name of Jesus.

46. O Lord, banish my enemies in my life for their many sins, in the name of Jesus.

47. My eyes grow weak with sorrow in the past, but now grow bright with joy, my enemies are confuse they fall apart, in the name of Jesus.

48. The wicked shall enter the gate of death and die, and they shall rise no more, in the name of Jesus.

49. Warriors of darkness that rise against me shall fail woefully, in the name of Jesus.

50. Every archer of Satan against me shall not stand his ground but fall, in the name of Jesus.

51. All fleet-footed soldiers around me shall be consumed and rise no more in the name of Jesus.

52. I shall declare praises to my Lord Almighty and my enemies shall rise no more, in the name of Jesus.

53. O Lord, crush my enemies, let them collapse and rise no more in the name of Jesus.

54. O Lord, let the enemy return to the grave and rise no more, in the name of Jesus.

55. O Lord, let my enemies be ashamed and dismayed, and turn back in sudden disgrace, in the name of Jesus.

56. Even in anger I shall not sin, so that the wicked will fall in the name of Jesus.

57. O Lord, destroy the wicked so that I laugh at them, in the name of Jesus.

58. O Lord, let the sword of the enemy pierce against their own heart, in the name of Jesus.

59. O Lord, let the wealth of the wicked disgrace them in the name of Jesus.

60. O Lord, break the power of the wicked, in the name of Jesus.

61. O Lord, let my enemy be empty in time of disaster, famine and time of harvest, in the name of Jesus.

62. Thou wicked that rise against me, perish, and vanish, like smoke, in the name of Jesus.

63. Thou wicked that borrow from me, in order to pay me with evil money, go blind and paralyze, in the name of Jesus.

64. Powers that want me to stumble on my way to progress, I fire you, die in the name of Jesus.

65. Those doing evil to captivate my life, meet double failure in the name of Jesus.
66. Any power that lie in wait to consume me, die, in the name of Jesus.
67. Thou wicked, that flourish in wickedness, your time is up, die in the name of Jesus.
68. O Lord, let me enjoy your fountain of life, and not the dread of enemy in the name of Jesus.
69. O Lord, erase anger in my life, so that enemy will not have upper hand in my life, in the name of Jesus.
70. O Lord, let every wicked scheme of the enemy, scatter, in the name of Jesus.
71. O Lord, give me justice against wicked plans of the enemy, in the name of Jesus.
72. O Lord, wear me with garment of righteousness, in the name of Jesus.
73. O Lord, let my righteousness put me ahead of my enemy, in the name of Jesus.
74. Warrior angels of God, be in fore front in battle to silence my enemy in the name of Jesus.
75. Supervising powers of my father's house, you shall rise no more, die, in the name of Jesus.
76. O Lord, arm me with strength to scatter the works of darkness, in the name of Jesus.
77. O Lord, pay back my enemy what they deserve, in the name of Jesus.

78. Every enemy that jubilate against me, be a failure and be rendered useless, in the name of Jesus.
79. O Lord, let the arrogance of the enemy work against them, in the name of Jesus.
80. O Lord, silence evildoers that boast against me, in the name of Jesus.

CHAPTER 5

I COMMAND FULL SCALE LAUGHTER AND PROSPERITY TO MY LIFE

Psalm 9:1-4

1. *I will give thanks to you, LORD, with all my heart; I will tell of all your wonderful deeds.*

2. *I will be glad and rejoice in you; I will sing the praises of your name, O Most High.*

3. *My enemies turn back; they stumble and perish before you.*

4. *For you have upheld my right and my cause, sitting enthroned as the righteous judge.*

Psalm 40:1-3

1. *I waited patiently for the LORD; he turned to me and heard my cry.*

2. *He lifted me out of the slimy pit, out of the mud and mire; he set my feet on a rock and gave me a firm place to stand.*

3. *He put a new song in my mouth, a hymn of praise to our God. Many will see and fear the LORD and put their trust in him.*

Isaiah 62:3-5

3. You will be a crown of splendor in the LORD's hand, a royal diadem in the hand of your God.

4. No longer will they call you Deserted, or name your land Desolate. But you will be called Hephzibah, and your land Beulah; for the LORD will take delight in you, and your land will be married.

5. As a young man marries a young woman, so will your Builder marry you; as a bridegroom rejoices over his bride, so will your God rejoice over you.

PRAYER POINTS

1. I thank you Lord, for your protection upon my life, in the name of Jesus.
2. I thank you Lord, for the full scale laughter that will fill my life in this prayer now and thereafter in the name of Jesus.
3. I thank you Lord, for the spirit of evangelism in my life in the name of Jesus.
4. I thank you Lord, for you are a covenant-keeping God in the name of Jesus.

5. I thank you Lord who removed my gaze on dark clouds and focus on your rainbow blessing in the name of Jesus.

6. Father Lord, give me thankful and loving heart, in the name of Jesus.

7. Lord Jesus, feed me with words of forgiveness in the name of Jesus.

8. O Lord, forgive me my sins and withdraw me from activities that brings sorrow in the name of Jesus.

9. Lord Jesus, empower me to hate sin with perfect hatred in the name of Jesus.

10. O Lord, do not let sin keep me down, in the name of Jesus.

11. Wind of God, blow sin away from my household in the name of Jesus.

12. O Lord, wear me with garment of righteousness, in the name of Jesus

13. I drink blood Jesus for fresh ideas to fill my heart and joy to be my food

14. I cover myself with blood of Jesus

15. Blood of Jesus, flow in my life, neutralize and destroy every deposit in my body in the name of Jesus

16. I spray eyes of monitoring spirit with blood of Jesus, and they are blind in the name of Jesus

17. Let blood of Jesus, speak and act for me in the spirit in the name of Jesus

18. I cover my surrounding and household with blood of Jesus

19. Holy Spirit, re-build and re-write my history today in the name of Jesus

20. Holy Spirit fill my heart with joy, in the name of Jesus

21. Holy Spirit, empower me to fear God and shun evil, in the name of Jesus

22. Holy Ghost, refresh and quicken my understanding, in the name of Jesus

23. Holy Spirit remove garment of sin from my life, wear me with garment of righteousness in the name of Jesus

24. Holy Spirit, hold me to yourself so that I may not grieve you, in the name of Jesus

25. My Lord shall make His way plain before my face, and I shall walk with Him, in the name of Jesus

26. The counsel of enemy against me shall not stand, I shall laugh over them, in the name of Jesus.

27. I praise you O LORD with all my heart for the wonders that happen in my life, in the name of Jesus.

28. I praise my God, who makes me glad and rejoice, in the name of Jesus.

29. I praise my God as my enemies stumble and rise no more, in the name of Jesus.

30. I praise my God, he uphold my right hand above my enemies, and burst into laughter and joy in the name of Jesus.

31. I praise my God, He rebuked my enemies, and they faint and turn back from pursuing me, in the name of Jesus.

32. I praise my God; He brought full scale laughter to me, and make endless ruin overtake my enemy in the name of Jesus.

33. I praise my God who erases memory of the wicked that rise up against me, in the name of Jesus.

34. I praise my God, who establishes His throne for judgment; I shall excel in judgment in the name of Jesus.

35. I command full scale laughter at enemies that persecute me, they failed in their enterprise against me in the name of Jesus.

36. I praise my God who turned to me and heard my cry for help and victory, in the name of Jesus.

37. I command full scale laugher and joy upon my life, as my God put a new song in my mouth, in the name of Jesus.
38. I praise my God, the blow of God scattered the face of my enemy, in the name of Jesus.
39. I command heavenly moth to consume the wealth of my enemy as they wish me in the spirit, in the name of Jesus.
40. I command joy and laughter into my life, as my God rescue me from strongmen and strongwomen, in the name of Jesus.
41. I command laughter and joy to my life as time of disaster is gone forever, in the name of Jesus.
42. I command laughter and joy to God, as I commit my life to Him, and Him only, in the name of Jesus.
43. I command laughter and joy to my life as ruthless enemies that rise up against me were put to shame.
44. I command laughter and joy to my life, as the prayer of my enemy came back unanswered, in the name of Jesus.
45. I command full scale laughter and joy for my life, the pit enemy dig for me become their lot in the name of Jesus.

46. I command full scale laughter and prosperity to my life, the net they hid for me caught them in the name of Jesus.

47. I command full scale laughter and prosperity to my life, the path of my enemy became dark and slippery in the name of Jesus.

48. I command full scale laughter and prosperity to my life, those who plan to disgrace me are put to shame, in the name of Jesus.

49. I command full scale laughter and prosperity to my life, those who seek my life, fail in their adventure, in the name of Jesus.

50. I command full scale laughter and prosperity to my life, my God fight against who fight against me, in the name of Jesus.

51. I command full scale laughter and prosperity to my life, and failure to my enemies who worship false gods in the name of Jesus.

52. I command full scale laughter and prosperity to my life, and fear no more in the name of Jesus.

53. O Lord, let many sorrow be to the wicked, and many joy to me, in the name of Jesus

54. O Lord, let the adversaries of the enemy meet concrete wall and scatter, in the name of Jesus

55. O Lord, open my eyes to the great joy I will experience in heaven, in the name of Jesus

56. I shall not waste time dwelling in the past that bring sorrow, in the name of Jesus
57. O Lord, let your amazing grace and peace rest upon me, in the name of Jesus
58. O Lord, favour me with grace and mercy in the name of Jesus
59. O Lord, with joy in my heart, let my household continue to honour you in the name of Jesus
60. O Lord, give me comfort and peace no one can take away, in the name of Jesus
61. O Lord, nourish my soul with food of heaven in the name of Jesus
62. O Lord, command your blessings upon me today, in the name of Jesus
63. My father and my God, shake the heavens and fill my life with wealth of wisdom, in the name of Jesus
64. Lord Jesus, as you love Jerusalem, show me love that abound
65. O Lord, multiply, the talents you entrusted in me to help humanity, in the name of Jesus
66. O Lord, enlarge my coast, cause laughter in my life, in the name of Jesus
67. O Lord, make me candidate of uncommon testimony in the name of Jesus
68. O Lord, empower me to possess the gates of my enemy, in the name of Jesus

69. O Lord, fight against them that fight against me, until they are defeated and end up in shame in the name of Jesus

70. I burn to ashes evil gift that cause sorrow in my life, in the name of Jesus

71. Problem expanders in the corridor of my life, enough is enough, expire in the name of Jesus

72. O Lord, render the habitation of darkness assign against me desolate, in the name of Jesus

73. O Lord, keep my feet from evil so that I may have peace in the name of Jesus

74. Thou that eat bread of wickedness and drink wine of violence, shall not find me out, in the name of Jesus

75. O Lord, remove curse from my life, in the name of Jesus

76. O Lord, let me inherit honour and be honoured everywhere I go in the name of Jesus. Amen

YOU HAVE BATTLES TO WIN
TRY THESE BOOKS

1. COMMAND THE DAY: DAILY PRAYER BOOK

Each day of the week is loaded with meanings and divine assurance. God did not create each day of the week for the fun of it. Blessings, success, gifts, resources, hopes, portfolios, duties, rights, prophecies, warnings and challenges, are loaded in each day.

Do you know the language, command or decree you can use to claim what belongs to you in each day of the week? Do you know in Christendom, Monday can be equated to one of the days of creation in Genesis chapter one? Do you know creation lasted for six days and God rested on the seventh day? What day of the week can Christian equate as the first day of the week, if we follow Christian calendar? What day can we call day seven?

This book shall give insight to these questions. It shall explain how you can command each day of the week according to creation in the book of Genesis chapter one.

Above all, you shall exercise your right and claim what is hidden in each day of the week.
Check for this in **COMMAND THE DAY: DAILY PRAYER BOOK**

2. PRAYER TO REMEMBER DREAMS

A lot of people are passing through this spiritual epidemic on a daily basis. Their dream life is epileptic, having no ability to remember all dreams they dream, or sometimes forget everything entirely. This is nothing but spiritual havoc you need to erase from your spiritual record.
The answer to every form of spiritual blackout

caused by spiritual erasers is found in, **PRAYER**

TO REMEMBER DREAMS

3. 100% CONFESSIONS AND PROPHECIES TO LOCATE HELPERS AND HELPERS TO LOCATE YOU

This is a wonderful book on confessions and prophecies to locate helpers and helpers to locate you. It is a prayer book loaded with over two thousand (2,000) prayer points.

The book unravels how to locate unknown helpers, prayers to arrest mind of helpers and prayers for manifestation after encounter with helpers.

4. ANOINTING FOR ELEVENTH HOUR HELP: HOPE AND HELP FOR YOUR TURBULENT TIMES

This book tells much of what to do at injury hour called eleventh hour. When you read and use this book as prescribed fear shall vanish in your life when pursuing a project, career or contract.

5. PRAYER TO LOCATE HELPERS AND HELPERS TO LOCATE YOU

Our divine helper is God. He created us to be together and be of help to one another. In the midst of no help we lost out, ending our journey in the wilderness.

There are keys assign to open right doors of life. You need right key to locate your helpers. Enough is enough; of suffering in silence.

With this book, you shall locate your helpers while your helpers shall locate you.

6. FIRE FOR FIRE PART ONE: (PRAYER BOOK BOOK 1)

This prayer book is fast at answering spiritual problems. It is a bulldozer prayer book, full of prayers all through. It is highly recommended for night vigil. Testimonies are pouring in daily from users of this book across the world!

7. PRAYER FOR FRUIT OF THE WOMB: EXPECTING MOTHERS

This prayer book is children magnet. By faith and believe in God Almighty, as soon as you use this book open doors to child bearing shall be yours. Amen

8. PRAYER FOR PREGNANT WOMEN: WITH ALL CHRISTIAN NAMES AND MEANINGS

This is a spiritual prayer book loaded with prayers of solution for pregnant women. As soon as you take in, the prayers you shall pray from day one of conception to the day of delivery are written in this book.

9. <u>WARFARE IN THE OFFICE: PRAYER</u> <u>TO SILENCE TOUGH TIMES IN OFFICE</u>

It is high time you pray prayers of power must change hands in office. Use this book and liberate yourself from every form of office yoke.

10. <u>MY MARRIAGE SHALL NOT BREAK:</u> <u>THE SECRET TO LOVE AND</u> <u>MARRIAGE THAT LASTS</u>

Marriage is corner piece of life, happiness and joy. You need to hold it tight and guide it from wicked intruders and destroyer of homes.

11. <u>VICTORY OVER SATANIC HOUSE</u> <u>PART ONE: RIDDING YOUR HOME OF</u> <u>SPIRITUAL DARKNESS</u>

Are you a tenant, Land lord bombarded left and right, front and back by wicked people around you?
With this book you shall be liberated from the hooks of the enemy.

12. <u>DICTIONARY OF DREAMS: THE</u> <u>DREAM INTERPRETATION</u>

DICTIONARY WITH SYMBOLS, SIGNS, AND MEANINGS

This is a must book for every home. It gives accurate details to about **10,000 (Ten thousand) dreams and interpretations,** written in alphabetical order for quick reference and easy digestion. The book portrays spiritual revelations with sound prophetic guidelines. It is loaded with Biblical references and violent prayers.
Ask for yours today.

For Further Enquiries Contact
THE AUTHOR
EVANGELIST TELLA OLAYERI
P.O. Box 1872 Shomolu Lagos.
Tel: 08023583168

FROM AUTHOR'S DESK
BEFORE YOU GO

Hello,

Thank you for purchasing this book. Would you consider posting a review about this book? In addition to providing feedback and arousing others into Christ's bosom, reviews can help other customers to know about the book.

Please take a minute to leave a review on this book.

I would appreciate that!

Thank you in advance, for your review and your patronage!!

Feel free to drop us your prayer request. We will join faith with you and God's power will be released in your life and issue in question.

http://tellaolayeri.com/prayerrequest.php

NOTE: You can get all my books from my website http://tellaolayeri.com

GOOD NEWS!!!

My audiobook is now available, to get one visit acx.com and search **"Tella Olayeri."**

Brethren, to be loaded and reloaded visit: amazon.com/author/tellaolayeri for a full spiritual sojourn for my books.

Thanks.

Made in the USA
Monee, IL
08 August 2023

40686108R00039

This is a book written to change destiny of people. It is a warfare prayer book that portrays you as a covenant child of God that must rise and shine. The peculiarity in you to prosper in faith, prosperity and to excel in life is well enshrined in this book.

This book ensures you pray into breakthrough and joy. The book breaks down your anatomy in prayer, build you in Christ and strengthen your relationship with God.

You may be a prayer warrior, praying with this book will add fire to your prayer altar. The prayer in this book is Holy Spirit vomited that will change your destiny. The prayers are well arranged by the spirit and are biblical.

They go straight to address the battles you face in Christian race and solution to it. At the end, enemies that rise against you shall surrender. It is by prayer this can be achieved, this is the reason this book is titled, "Prayer that makes enemy surrender"

This book shall establish your relationship with God, cover your nakedness and ensure you recover all you lost to Satan in the past. No matter how draconian enemies may be, they will lose and be powerless over your situation.

The God of Abraham, Isaac and Jacob shall arise in gap for you. No power of darkness shall have a say any more in your situation. The battle is half won as you read and pray with this book.

It is time to give thanks to God more than before. You can only if your enemies surrender. This is the book you need most to achieve this. Endeavor you pick this book and sail through the of life.
Pick it and match on as a champion.